Published by Rock N' Roll Colouring Ltd® 2021

© 2021 Iron Maiden LLP. Iron Maiden ® Under License to Global Merchandising Services Ltd

Designer: Mark Leary at Asylumseventy7

All rights reserved. No portion of this book may be reproduced, stored in a retrieval system, or transmitted in any form or by any means, mechanical, electronic, photocopying, recording, or otherwise, without permission from the publisher.

Based on the illustrations by Derek Riggs, Melvyn Grant, Herve Monjeaud and Mark Wilkinson

First published in the UK by Rock N' Roll Colouring Ltd®
London
www.rocknrollcolouring.com

ISBN: 978 1 8381470 5 1

Printed in the UK by W&G Baird

The Official Iron Maiden Colouring Book

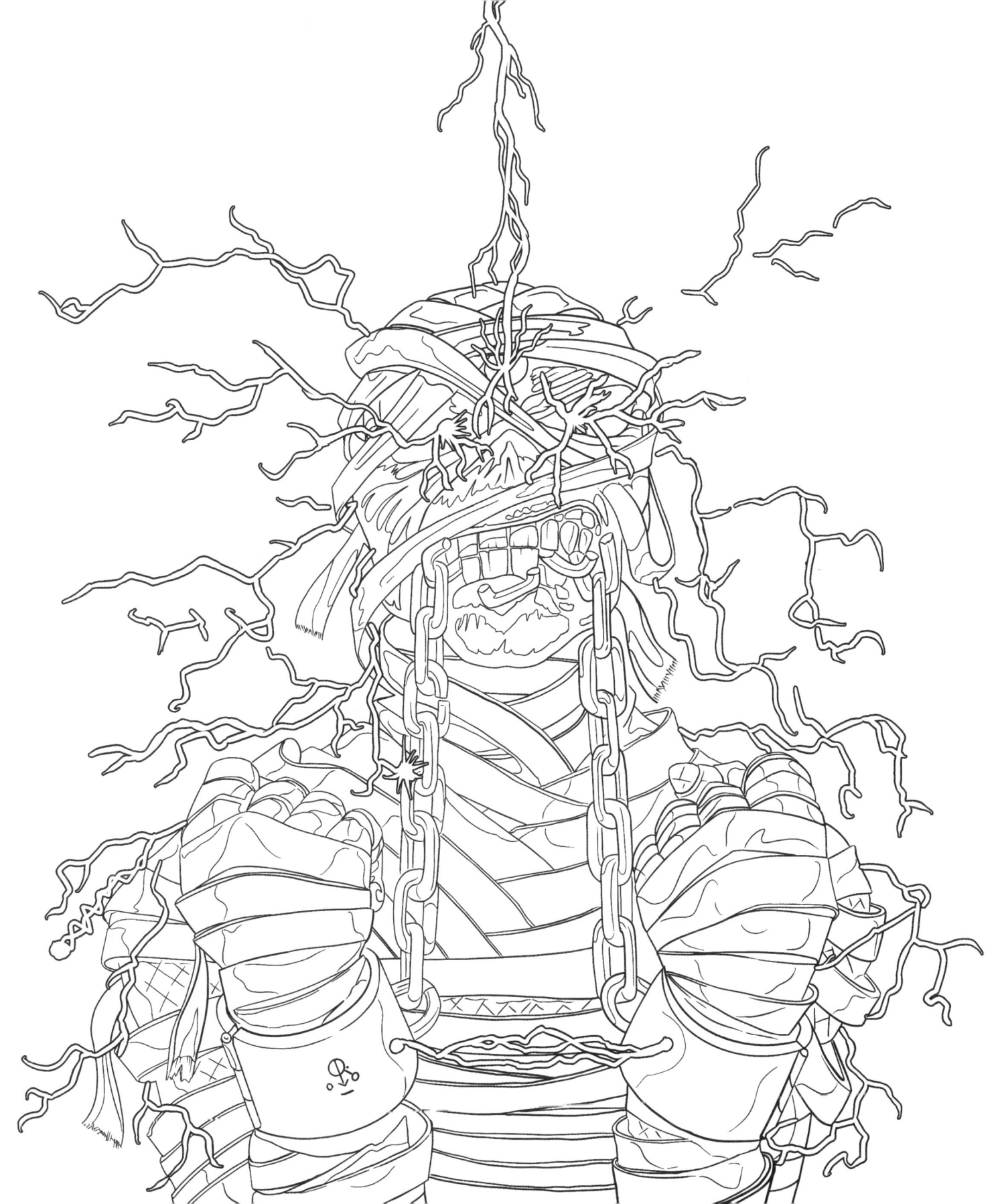

For your doodles